Animal TECH

WINGS & BEAKS

Tessa Miller

full tilt PRESS

Wings & Beaks
Animal Tech

Full Tilt Press
42982 Osgood Road
Fremont, CA 94539
readfulltilt.com

Full Tilt Press publications may be purchased for educational, business, or sales promotional use.

Editorial Credits
Design and layout by Sara Radka
Edited by Renae Gilles
Copyedited by Kristin J. Russo

Image Credits
Book Buddy Media: 17 (helmet diagram); Getty Images: cover, Andrey Davidenko, 38, Antagain, 32 (dragonfly), 33 (dragonfly), Blend Images, 37, 44, Brand X, 13, DNY59, 15 (helmet), Dorling Kindersley RF, 15 (diagram), 29 (sonar diagram), Flickr RF, 24, 36, FrankRamspott, 40 (diagram), GA161076, 21 (trains), iStockphoto, 5, 9, 12, 18, 19, 26, 30, 39, 41, 10 (bird), 14 (top), 16 (diagram), 16 (woodpecker), 21 (kingfisher), 22 (kingfisher diving), 22 (kingfisher on branch), 23 (train), 28 (bat), 34 (dragonfly), 40 (honeybee), background, James Pinsky/U.S. Navy, 27, Jeff J Mitchell, 42, Kristian1108, 11 (airplane), Manny Ceneta, 43, Moment Open, 14 (bottom), Moment RF, 4, 20, 31, 34 (dragonfly eyes), 35 (camera lens), 35 (drone), 41 (smartphone), Nastasic, 6, paci77, 45, scanrail, 23 (train drawing), Sean Gallup, 33 (micro quadcopter), View Stock RF, 17 (race car driver); Newscom: Album / Gus Regalado, 28 (echolocation diagram), CB2/ZOB/NOAA Office of National Marine S, 29 (sunken ship), The Print Collector / Heritage-Images, 8, ZCHE/Ortega, 25; Pixabay: cover; Shutterstock: cover, Elena Ray, 10 (x-ray); Wikimedia: 8, Arne Nordmann, 11 (diagram), Central Intelligence Agency, 32 (insectohopter), Wilbur Wright and Orville Wright, 7

ISBN: 978-1-62920-736-0 (library binding)
ISBN: 978-1-62920-776-6 (eBook)

CONTENTS

The study of bees has improved many things, including wide-angle cameras and a new type of rubber.

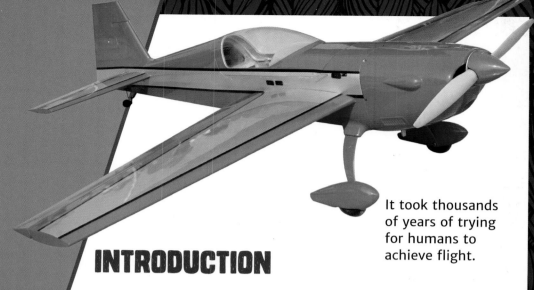

It took thousands of years of trying for humans to achieve flight.

INTRODUCTION

People have been dreaming about flying like birds since ancient times. Artists from thousands of years ago carved figures of humans with wings. These pieces of art show us how long humans have dreamed of flying. Scientists have made this dream possible, with the help of a few feathered friends. Today, birds still play a large part in flying. Now, more than 8 million people fly in planes every day.

Scientists and **engineers** have many problems to solve. They sometimes look to animals and nature for answers. This is called biomimicry. Bio means "life." "Mimicry" is when you copy something else.

Airplanes are one of the most well-known examples of biomimicry. But biomimicry has allowed a lot of **technology** to move forward. It has helped make new, exciting things possible. Airplanes, trains, and sonar are all inventions that have been improved with biomimicry. There are many more fascinating examples. Read on to learn how looking to nature has changed our world.

---

engineer: a person who plans and builds tools, machines, or structures

technology: tools and knowledge used to meet a need or solve a problem

BIRDS

AIRPLANES

Gulls move their wings to soar, dive, twist, and snatch a fish to eat.

The Wright brothers made wings that could twist at the pilot's command, just like bird wings.

On December 17, 1903, brothers Orville and Wilbur Wright made history. They flew the first airplane. Their first flight was only 12 seconds long. They flew 120 feet (36.5 meters). This might not sound like a big deal today. But at the time, it was ground-breaking technology. Other flying machines had relied on the wind to move. They could go only in the direction the wind was blowing. The Wright brothers **designed** a plane that flew without the help of the wind or pedals to move. Their plane also had controls that let them steer it in any direction.

The Wright brothers spent many years doing **research** before they flew. They watched different types of birds. They built gliders by mimicking birds' wings. A glider is a type of flying machine without an engine. Gliders fly by using wind to hold them up in the air. The Wright brothers built more than 100 gliders. Each glider had a different shape of wing. The Wright brothers **experimented** many times. Finally they found a wing design that allowed them to fly.

---

design: to make a plan by thinking about the purpose or use of something

research: detailed study of a particular topic

experiment: to test; to try different things to discover what works

LESSONS FROM NATURE

People have been inspired by birds in flight for thousands of years. In ancient China, people built kites in the shapes of birds and bats. They were fascinated by the heavens. In 1783, two brothers in France invented the hot air balloon. Finally, people could see the world from a bird's-eye view. In 1799, George Cayley designed and flew the first gliders. The wings were shaped like a bird's wings. But they did not flap. Cayley's gliders were the first flying machines to carry a person. The first person to ever fly was a 10-year-old boy, in 1849.

George Cayley

George Cayley designed gliders big enough to carry the weight of a person through the air.

Owls have special feathers that change the flow of air and reduce noise. People are now trying to build airplanes with similar features.

The Wright brothers' plane from 1903 heavily influenced the design of **modern** planes. A new plane called the "Dreamliner" has wings made out of a special type of plastic. This plastic bends and moves with air **currents**. It works just as a bird's wings do. This

DID YOU KNOW?

Scientists think the first bird was a dinosaur named Archaeopteryx. It was the size of a raven and had sharp claws and teeth.

makes flying in the plane less bumpy when the air currents have sudden changes. Those changes are called turbulence. Today we depend on airplanes for transportation and **industry**. There are at least 5,000 airplanes in the air every minute of the day. Biomimicry allows these planes to fly faster, more quietly, and more safely.

modern: up-to-date; from current or recent times

current: a flow of air or water in one direction

industry: the action of making something by using machines and factories

TECH IN ACTION

From early gliders to the jumbo jets flown today,
airplane technology has been greatly influenced by birds.

FEATHERS
Birds' feathers help them fly. They also help birds change directions.

BEAK
A pointed beak helps a bird fly faster by "cutting" the air in front of it.

BONES
Birds have hollow bones. This makes them very light.

RUDDERS
Planes have rudders that help them change directions.

NOSE
A pointed nose lets a plane fly through the air quickly and smoothly.

WINGS
The wings of a plane are hollow. This makes planes lightweight.

N1186T

WOODPECKERS

SHOCK ABSORBERS

Woodpeckers can withstand impacts that are 10 times stronger than the average car crash.

Scientists have been using crash test dummies since the 1980s. This way, they can test parts like shock absorbers safely.

Have you ever ridden in a car on a bumpy road? Why can you feel only the biggest bumps? It is because cars have shock absorbers. Shock absorbers are springs attached to the car's wheels. These springs act like cushions. They **absorb** bumps. This makes the car ride smoother. If cars did not have shock absorbers, drivers would have a hard time controlling the cars as they jumped. They would probably crash.

The best shock absorbers in nature belong to the woodpecker. These birds use their beaks to punch holes in trees. They use the holes to find their prey. Woodpeckers also drum on things, such as trees or buildings. This is how they talk to each other. Scientists want to know how woodpeckers can do this. They hit their heads against hard objects without hurting their brains. This would be helpful when designing better shock absorbers for people.

absorb: to prevent something harmful or unwanted from passing through

Woodpeckers drill into trees to reach food, mostly insects.

LESSONS FROM NATURE

Woodpeckers can pound their heads into trees about 12,000 times a day. They do not get hurt. They can do this because the bones in their heads are very soft. They cushion the woodpecker's brain when it hits the inside of the **skull**.

Woodpeckers usually don't kill a tree, but they can damage it.

skull: the bones of an animal's face and head

Scientists in the United Kingdom are mimicking the bones of woodpeckers' skulls. They want to make safety helmets for people. They designed a new type of cardboard. Then they put the cardboard inside bike helmets. It works better than normal helmets. Those have a layer of thick, hard foam. When taking a hit, the layer of foam is crushed. But the new cardboard has special air pockets. They absorb the force of a hit, rather than being crushed like the foam. Now people want to use this cardboard in helmets of all types. That includes those for football players and racecar drivers.

Scientists studying woodpeckers have also designed a new type of metal. This metal is a lot like the bone of the woodpecker's skull. It has layers with spaces in between. The spaces are filled with glass marbles. They absorb energy. People are looking at ways to put it in body armor. This may help save the lives of soldiers when they get shot.

A woodpecker's head and beak are connected differently from other birds' heads and beaks. The head and beak are separated by a spongy bone that acts like a shock absorber.

DID YOU KNOW?
A woodpecker can hit a tree 18–20 times per second.

Football helmets reduce the risk of brain injuries, but players can still get seriously hurt.

TECH IN ACTION

The woodpecker's unique body has inspired better materials for shock absorbers.

SKULL
The soft bones of a woodpecker's skull cushion the brain.

BONE
A special bone in the woodpecker's head acts like a seatbelt. It holds the brain in place.

AIR HOLES
Tiny air holes in the woodpecker's skull help break up the force of pecking a tree.

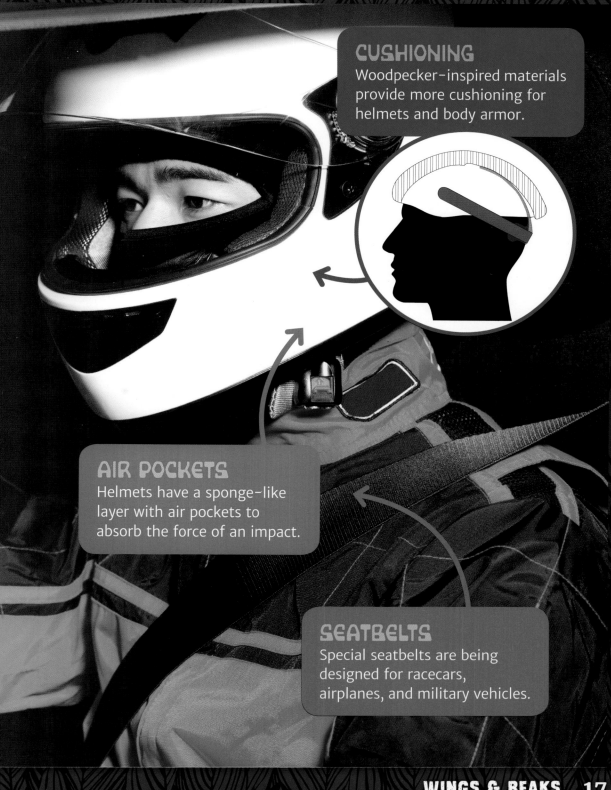

CUSHIONING
Woodpecker-inspired materials provide more cushioning for helmets and body armor.

AIR POCKETS
Helmets have a sponge-like layer with air pockets to absorb the force of an impact.

SEATBELTS
Special seatbelts are being designed for racecars, airplanes, and military vehicles.

KINGFISHERS

BULLET TRAINS

A kingfisher spends 80 percent of its day hunting. All that practice has made it very good at diving for fish and other food.

Bullet trains now connect many of Japan's major cities.

A kingfisher is another bird scientists are studying. The shape of a kingfisher's head and beak are unique. Imagine diving into water without making a splash. A kingfisher can.

The kingfisher's beak is in the shape of a **wedge**. This lets the bird enter the water without making a wave. Its dives are almost silent. It leaves the water undisturbed. This is important for when the kingfisher is sneaking up on a fish to eat it.

Now imagine a train that can travel up to 200 miles (320 kilometers) per hour. It doesn't make a sound. Impossible, right? Not anymore. Engineers in Japan have designed bullet trains. These trains travel very smoothly. The air barely moves around them as they speed by. To achieve this, engineers studied kingfishers. The nose of a bullet train is shaped like the beak of a kingfisher. The train can travel without making a sound. Its shape helps it cut quietly through the air, like how a kingfisher can dive without making a splash.

---

wedge: an object is thick on one end, and thin and pointed on the other

Most trains travel up to 80 miles (130 km) per hour. To make trains go faster than that, engineers had to change the shape of the front of a train from a square to a wedge.

LESSONS FROM NATURE

Normal trains have fronts that are round or square. They do not cut through the air. They push the air out of the way. When engineers were designing the bullet train, they realized that a normal train nose slowed the bullet train down. It also made a lot of noise when the bullet train left a tunnel. This is because of air pressure. The air pressure outside of a tunnel is low. But the pressure inside a tunnel is high. This makes it harder for a train to keep up its speed when going through a tunnel.

Japanese engineer Eiji Nakatsu and his team tested different nose shapes. They couldn't build a lot of trains. So they tested smaller objects first. They built special bullets. Then they shot them through a pipe. They dropped them into water. Then they recorded the splash. Advanced computers ran many tests on the possible shapes. The shape that did the best was the wedge of the kingfisher's beak. The research team then used that same shape to build the nose of the bullet train. It worked.

Kingfishers can dive up to 25 miles (40 km) per hour.

DID YOU KNOW?

Engineers in Texas are building a track for a Japanese bullet train to connect the cities of Dallas and Houston. This train would travel at 205 miles (330 km) per hour.

Bullet trains require less money, gas, and electricity to run. This means they are better for the environment too.

TECH IN ACTION

The kingfisher moves with great speed. Thanks to biomimicry, the bullet train does too.

HEAD
The wedge shape of a kingfisher's head helps it dive into water without a splash.

MOVEMENT
The kingfisher's shape allows it to move from low-pressure air to high-pressure water easily.

ANGLE
The angle the kingfisher uses to dive also prevents splashing.

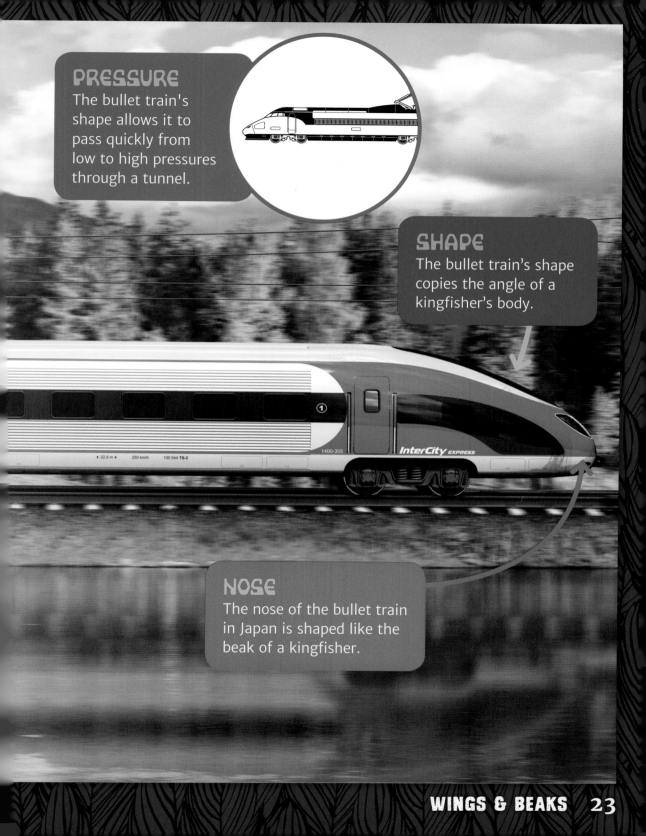

PRESSURE

The bullet train's shape allows it to pass quickly from low to high pressures through a tunnel.

SHAPE

The bullet train's shape copies the angle of a kingfisher's body.

NOSE

The nose of the bullet train in Japan is shaped like the beak of a kingfisher.

InterCity EXPRESS

1400-305

► 22.5 m ◄   250 km/h   130 044 TS-2

BATS

SONAR

Most of the sounds bats make when flying and hunting are too high for humans to hear.

Sonar stands for Sound Navigation And Ranging. Ranging means moving around an area, like a bat does while hunting.

Birds are not the only flying animals scientists have turned to for answers. Bats are flying **mammals**. They use echolocation. This lets them **navigate** and hunt in the dark. Echolocation works by using sound. A bat first makes many high-pitched sounds. The sounds bounce off things. The bat then measures how long it takes the echoes to come back. This way, the bat can tell how far away something is. Echolocation lets bats fly around quickly. It also lets them find food in the dark.

Sonar is based on echolocation. It works the same way. But it is used underwater, where it is too dark to see. Militaries in the United States and Europe have been using sonar since the early 1900s. They use sonar to navigate safely through dangerous places. This includes underwater mine fields. They also use it to track torpedoes from enemy ships. When not at war, sonar is used on submarines to find sunken ships and airplanes that have crashed into the ocean. Sonar is very important. Scientists are always looking for ways to improve it.

mammal: a warm-blooded animal with hair or fur that gives birth to live young and feeds its young milk

navigate: to find a route when traveling, usually by using a map

LESSONS FROM NATURE

Bats are not the only animals to use echolocation. Dolphins, porpoises, and other toothed whales use it as well. These animals are able to **process** many sounds coming at them very quickly. This lets them tell the difference between objects that are close together. Dolphins can locate fish that are hidden in sand. Bats can pick out a single insect from a swarm.

Using echolocation, bats can tell the size, speed, direction, and distance of another animal or object.

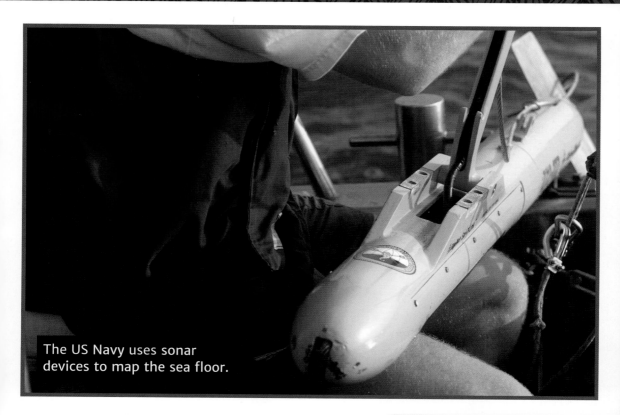

The US Navy uses sonar devices to map the sea floor.

Sonar already works very well. Advanced computers can single out echoes that are very close together. The echoes are only 12 millionths of a second apart. But bats can do it better. They can single out echoes that are 2 millionths of a second apart. Military engineers are designing better sonar **systems** because of this research. The military wants to make its sonar as good as bat echolocation. Then it could locate objects that are separated by the width of a human hair.

DID YOU KNOW?
People first built sonar systems to detect icebergs. Sonar was then used during World War I (1914–1918) to locate enemy submarines.

process: to receive, organize, and use information

system: a set of parts that work together

TECH IN ACTION

Bats are experts at using sound to find and identify objects while flying. They are inspiring better sonar for use underwater.

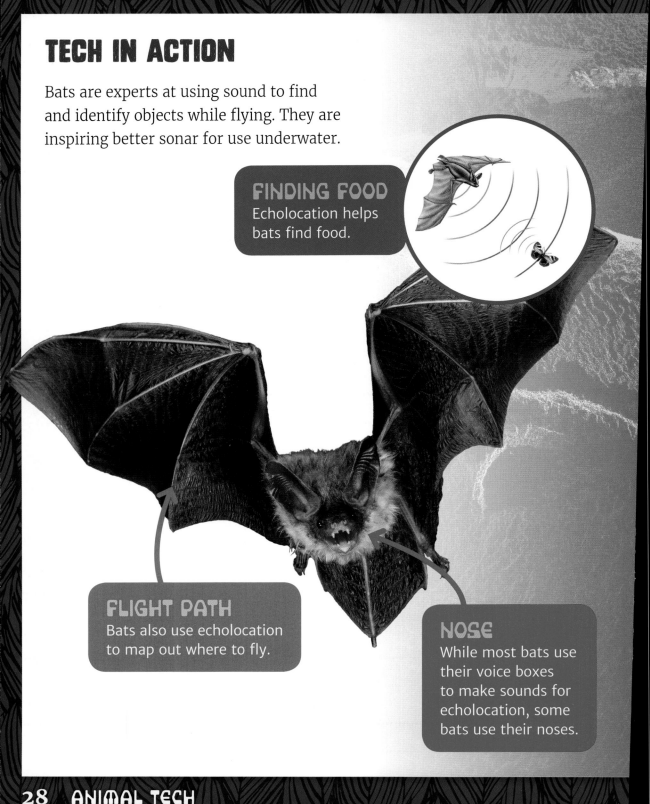

FINDING FOOD
Echolocation helps bats find food.

FLIGHT PATH
Bats also use echolocation to map out where to fly.

NOSE
While most bats use their voice boxes to make sounds for echolocation, some bats use their noses.

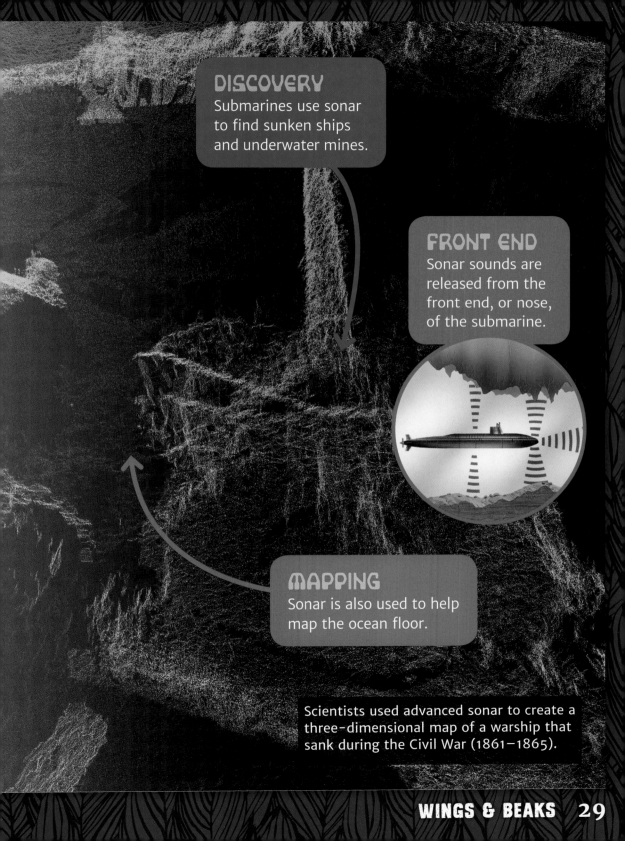

DISCOVERY
Submarines use sonar to find sunken ships and underwater mines.

FRONT END
Sonar sounds are released from the front end, or nose, of the submarine.

MAPPING
Sonar is also used to help map the ocean floor.

Scientists used advanced sonar to create a three-dimensional map of a warship that sank during the Civil War (1861–1865).

DRAGONFLIES

DRONES

Some large dragonflies can fly
up to 40 miles (64 km) per hour.

Many small aircraft have four "wings," mimicking the four wings of a dragonfly.

Imagine you are a spy on a secret mission. You need to gather information from your enemy. But when you get too close, they see you and run away. How are you going to sneak up on them without being seen?

Now imagine a **drone** so small it fits in your pocket. This drone can fly into your enemy's hideout without being seen. The drone is speedy, small, and silent. What does it look like? If you imagined it looks like a dragonfly, you are right.

Today, researchers and engineers in the United States are making drones. They fly just like a dragonfly. The dragonfly is a good animal to mimic. It has four wings. They move independently. This lets the dragonfly move straight up and down and hover in one place. It can also move backward and change directions very quickly.

drone: an aircraft that can fly without a pilot on board

The 1970s dragonfly insectothopter was crafted by a watchmaker. It had a miniature engine that powered its wings.

LESSONS FROM NATURE

The Central Intelligence Agency (CIA) has already made dragonfly-inspired drones. Engineers in the 1970s designed small flying spies. They were called insectothopters. But the insectothopters were unable to fly in windy conditions. So the CIA gave up on the project.

DID YOU KNOW?

Dragonflies are the best hunters in the animal kingdom. Their hunts are successful 95 percent of the time. Lions catch only 20 percent of the animals they hunt.

Today researchers have made these drones better. They started looking more closely at dragonflies. Dragonflies fly silently. They can move in any direction. They can see almost completely around themselves. Researchers have studied these abilities. They have made many improvements on the insectothopter. The new drones are called **micro** air vehicles (MAVs). Some look just like dragonflies.

MAVs can be used in schools to help students learn about flight. They can take pictures in dangerous places after a disaster. MAVs also make excellent tools for spy missions.

micro: very small

As drones become more common, they are causing a few problems. Some people are using drones to spy on famous people and to hunt illegally.

TECH IN ACTION

Forty years after the CIA mimicked dragonflies to design drones, researchers are perfecting their work.

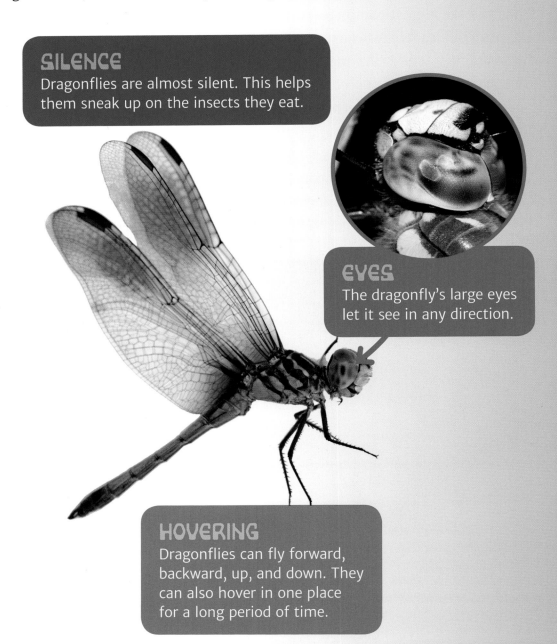

SILENCE
Dragonflies are almost silent. This helps them sneak up on the insects they eat.

EYES
The dragonfly's large eyes let it see in any direction.

HOVERING
Dragonflies can fly forward, backward, up, and down. They can also hover in one place for a long period of time.

SURVEILLANCE
Drones are often used to hover over areas in order to capture video or photos of anything that may be moving below them.

QUIET
MAVs are as quiet as dragonflies.

CAMERA
MAVs have cameras that let them take pictures from any direction.

BEES

DELIVERY APP

To make 1 cup (240 milliliters) of honey, bees fly about 40,000 miles (64,000 km) in search of flowers.

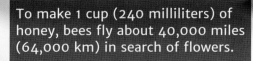

A delivery driver might make 100 stops in one day.

Imagine you are a delivery driver. You are trying to drop off hundreds of packages in a single day. How are you supposed to get them all to the right place by the right time? What if you get lost?

Delivery companies in the US have been trying to become more **efficient** for 50 years. Recently, they decided to hire math experts to help them. These experts made computer programs. They are able to plan efficient **routes**. But these computer programs are very expensive. Only the largest companies can afford them.

Thankfully, a company named Routific has made a phone **app**. It does the same thing. The app mimics how bees find the best flowers for making honey. Bees have a system that is very efficient. Now any delivery driver can use the app. They can map out the most efficient delivery route. Small companies that deliver items such as food or flowers can use it. This helps them save both time and money.

---

efficient: able to succeed without wasting time or materials

route: the path taken to get from one place to another

app: a small computer program, usually downloaded to a mobile device

LESSONS FROM NATURE

The app works by using "the bee's algorithm." An algorithm is a set of steps used to solve a math problem. The bee's algorithm copies how bees find the best flowers. Bees send out their fastest fliers first. These fast bees fly in random directions in search of flowers. Then they take the most direct way back to the hive. At the hive, they do a special dance. It is called the "waggle dance." The dance tells the other bees how to find the best flowers. When those bees return, they let the others know if they found an even better route.

During the waggle dance, a bee describes a flower's distance and direction from the hive. The longer the bee dances, the farther the flower is from the hive.

A driver making 25 stops can choose from 50 trillion possible routes.

Using the bee's algorithm, each delivery truck is treated like a bee. Each delivery stop is treated like a flower. The app sends out a group of digital "trucks." The "trucks" start finding routes to take. The app then **analyzes** how efficient the routes are. If the app finds a good route, it does its own "waggle dance." It sends more "trucks." It then compares the different route options. Once the app finds the most efficient route, it tells the user. This task takes the app a few minutes. It would take a person all day to do it by hand.

analyze: to study something closely and carefully

TECH IN ACTION

In this example of biomimicry, the delivery trucks are the bees and the customers are the flowers.

SPEED
Bees send out their fastest fliers to find the best flowers.

FOCUS
When bees find a spot with lots of good flowers, they send many bees to the area.

DANCE
Honeybees dance in front of other bees to tell them where the best flowers are.

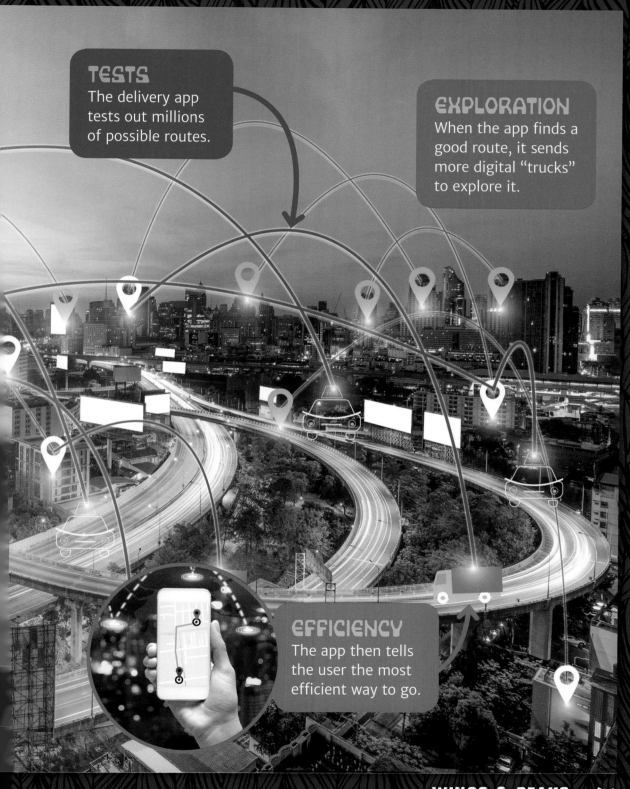

TESTS
The delivery app tests out millions of possible routes.

EXPLORATION
When the app finds a good route, it sends more digital "trucks" to explore it.

EFFICIENCY
The app then tells the user the most efficient way to go.

WINGS & BEAKS

CONCLUSION

When flying in formation, geese are better able to keep track of one another.

Fighter pilots flying in formation have better safety, efficiency, and communication.

Winged animals have taught scientists and engineers a lot. Planes, trains, and delivery trucks are now faster and more efficient. This helps save people a lot of time. It also saves gas. Saving gas helps the environment, as well.

All of these **innovations** make people's lives better. Some technologies, such as better helmets and seatbelts, may even save lives. Soldiers working with improved sonar and drones help make the world a safer place.

Right now, engineers are studying geese flying in "V" formations. One day they hope planes will be able to fly together like this. This will help planes save even more fuel. They will fly even faster. There are also multiple companies working on making dragonfly drones. They will be for people to buy, not just for the military. Can you imagine where biomimicry could take us next? All you have to do is look to the sky for inspiration.

---

innovation: a new and creative idea, solution, or product

ACTIVITY

PROTECT THE "BRAIN"

Have you ever wondered how helmets protect your head? What materials are used? How far can a helmet fall before it breaks? Here is a fun activity to see if you can figure out a way to help protect your brain better. In this experiment, you will try to save an egg from cracking after it is dropped.

WHAT YOU NEED

- A helpful adult with a ladder
- Hard-boiled eggs
- Bike or other sports helmets
- Tape, glue, or string
- Scissors
- Protective materials, such as sponges, cardboard, and bubble wrap

WHAT TO DO

1. Study your helmet. Write down what you think keeps your head from getting hurt. Brainstorm how each part of the helmet works and why it is there.

2. Next, take a look at the "Woodpeckers & Shock Absorbers" chapter of this book, on pages 12 to 17. With the woodpecker in mind, make a design that you think will make the helmet better.

3. Using the protective materials, build your new helmet around your egg "brain." Make sure to be gentle with the egg.

4. Have an adult drop your protected egg from low on the ladder. If the egg doesn't break, try dropping it from higher up the ladder. How high can it go before it breaks?

5. What do you think kept the egg safe? What let the egg crack? Brainstorm what you think worked and what didn't. You can use your results to design an improved helmet.

6. Clean up the mess!

GLOSSARY

absorb: to prevent something harmful or unwanted from passing through

analyze: to study something closely and carefully

app: a small computer program, usually downloaded to a mobile device

current: a flow of air or water in one direction

design: to make a plan by thinking about the purpose or use of something

drone: an aircraft that can fly without a pilot on board

efficient: able to succeed without wasting time or materials

engineer: a person who plans and builds tools, machines, or structures

experiment: to test; to try different things to discover what works

industry: the action of making something by using machines and factories

innovation: a new and creative idea, solution, or product

mammal: a warm-blooded animal with hair or fur that gives birth to live young and feeds its young milk

micro: very small

modern: up-to-date; from current or recent times

navigate: to find a route when traveling, usually by using a map

process: to receive, organize, and use information

research: detailed study of a particular topic

route: the path taken to get from one place to another

skull: the bones of an animal's face and head

system: a set of parts that work together

technology: tools and knowledge used to meet a need or solve a problem

wedge: an object is thick on one end, and thin and pointed on the other

READ MORE

Gregory, Josh. *From Woodpeckers to . . . Helmets.* Innovations from Nature. Ann Arbor, Mich.: Cherry Lake Publishing, 2013.

Holzweiss, Kristina. *Amazing Makerspace DIY Fliers.* New York: Children's Press, 2018.

Lee, Dora. *Biomimicry.* Toronto: Kids Can Press, 2011.

Rothman, Julia. *Nature Anatomy: The Curious Parts and Pieces of the Natural World.* North Adams, Mass.: Storey Publishing, 2015.

Stewart, Melissa. *Feathers: Not Just for Flying.* Watertown, Mass.: Charlesbridge, 2014.

WEBSITES

https://www.natgeokids.com/nz/discover/animals/insects/honey-bees/#!/register
Read 10 more facts about bees.

www.pbs.org/wgbh/nova/next/body/bioinspired-assistive-devices
Learn about a bat-inspired example of biomimicry.

https://rangerrick.org/ranger_rick/flying-aces/
Read a comic about fascinating birds, such as falcons and vultures.

http://www.greeneducationfoundation.org/resources/Amtrak/Amtrak.html
Watch a cartoon on inventions that came from biomimicry.

INDEX